HOW TO SPOT
A DINOSAUR

HOW TO SPOT A DINOSAUR

or

How to Survive and Thrive in the Workplace

Susie Kay

and

Kathy Ennis

Illustrations by Rebecca Walters

PROFESSIONALISM BOOKS

HOW TO SPOT A DINOSAUR?

or

How to Survive and Thrive in the Workplace

Originally published in Great Britain in 2014

www.theprofessionalismgroup.co.uk/dinosaur

ISBN 978-0-9565401-2-6 Print edition

Printed in the United Kingdom

To the memory of Carl Linnaeus
because God created but Linnaeus organised!

'Deus creavit, Linnaeus deposuit'

Carl Linnaeus was an 18th Century Swedish botanist, physician and zoologist, who laid the foundations for the modern scheme of binomial nomenclature. He is known as the father of modern taxonomy and is also considered one of the fathers of modern ecology. He was one of the first scientists to regard man as an integral part of the natural world.
He named us Homo sapiens in 1758.

CONTENTS

ELEPHANT HORDE

LION

POSSE

PACK

MISCHIEF MOVEMENT HERD MOLE
SKULK BAND MONKEY
CHARACTERISTICS MOB
OWL TURKEY OWL PERSONALITY COMMITTEE RAFT TRIP
COMMITTEE WISDOM
SWAN
VULTURE LEASH HYENA DROVE TROOP FLOCK MISCHIEF CACKLE
OSTRICH DINOSAUR PACK COLONY
COMPANY ELEPHANT VULTURE OSTRICH BAND VULTURE CLAN PACE
CLAN DINOSAUR PARADE
TRIBE HERD PARLIAMENT MOVEMENT FLOCK LABOUR
PRIDE BEAVER MONKEY
SHEEP NEST FOX COLONY CACKLE COLD N Y
VENUE
BANK MOB TROOP FLOCK
FAMILY
SHREWDNESS
SHREWDNESS HARVEST MOLE

WHAT'S IT ALL ABOUT?

Way back in the early noughties, we were due to run a series of workshops on the dynamics of work based relationships and its effect on professional development.

In our preparation discussions we started to describe the personal characteristics of people we had met over the years and realised that they were starting to fall into some very interesting categories. What's more, we could describe those categories by labelling them with the name of an animal - because the perceived characteristics of the animal and the individuals we were describing were incredibly similar.

Much riotous laughter later, we realised that we had hit on an interesting and serious problem for many people in trying to deal with all the different personality types encountered within the work environment and the problems some of these interactions can cause.

Although many trees have been sacrificed to inform us about the range of management and personality theories which might explain these issues there is not, of course, any scientific basis to our current zoological-inspired offering. This begins as a light hearted trawl through the issues of personality types, staff engagement and team building - including how to value all contributions from different work personalities- but continues by recognising where the challenges are likely to come from and how to survive them! We then move on to offer some assistance on how to survive and thrive in your workplace, regardless of whether you are a solo entrepreneur, an employee of companies or organisations of any size or, indeed, a manager attempting to bring harmony and effectiveness to your teams.

So, in an effort to be helpful, here are the animal types we have identified and their various characteristics. We guarantee that as you read through you will start to recognise yourself and to think of colleagues past and present – but we recommend you keep it to yourself!

Susie Kay and Kathy Ennis
London
January 2014

KEY

Throughout the book we are using some symbols as a shorthand way of pointing your attention at something to remember or something that would be useful for you to do.

So keep your eyes open for the symbols we are using:

 Quotes – obviously!

 Top hints or tips worth remembering

 A series of steps through an activity

 A question we are asking you to consider

 A very worthwhile exercise for you to do
Yoda says "Do or do not...there is no try!"

All of our charts and exercises are available as free downloads at
www.theprofessionalismgroup.co.uk/dinosaur

WHY IS IT USEFUL?

We live in a very uncertain world

If the last three or four years have taught us anything, it is that current economic uncertainties mean that nothing is more certain than change, then more change, then a bit more and on it goes. However much we plan, some days can take us completely by surprise and often these types of days are the result of someone else's planning or actions, over which we have little or no control. So we definitely cannot ignore what is happening around us and hope that everything will be OK. Burying one's head in the sand and hoping for a great outcome, a bit like an ostrich, is very unlikely to achieve the desired result.

What's the problem?

So, as the pace of change accelerates and redundancies and staff reshuffles occur more frequently, it is quite possible to find ourselves in a work environment where the wrong assortment of personalities has resulted in the creation of a badly mixed team, creating stress and impeding the pace and flow of work.

We may walk into them as the result of getting a new job or moving into a new role; we may create them by reorganising the current workforce; we may inherit them by taking over or joining an existing team or, as interims or freelancers and entrepreneurs, we may walk into an unknown environment with a range of complete strangers whom we need to assess very rapidly in order to complete our work effectively. As a new entrepreneur we may find ourselves in situations which are unfamiliar or struggle to work with people or situations where we feel somewhat uncomfortable.

You may quickly become very aware that there is something wrong, an issue that needs dealing with, but what is it that's causing the problem? These uncomfortable teams or relationships can be caused by having the wrong people in particular roles, attempting to pull the wrong combination of people into a functional team or just trying to work in new situations or circumstances.

It's Workplace Stress – or something like it

Workplace stress gets in the way of progress, takes up valuable time and can create deeply dysfunctional work environments. Seemingly insurmountable problems take up valuable time, eating away at your ability to deliver your role, by intruding the need for a solution when you just want to get on and do your job.

Understanding who and what

So how do we find a way out of this potential minefield? Well, in the first instance, there are many benefits which derive from understanding the various personality types around you, not the least of which is gaining valuable insights into how you personally react to and deal with the situations and the people you encounter.

After that, it is about understanding the effect that stress can have on you and the people around you and we will deal with that in a later chapter.

Team leader, team member or solo – it doesn't matter

Whether you are managing an organisation, are a team leader, a member of the team or a sole trader, you need to be able to work out how the various personalities around you contribute to the overall interactions you are experiencing or, sadly, to the problems you may be facing.

Our hope is that your enhanced understanding of the complexities of expectations from all sides will allow you to improve the way you communicate with those around you, minimize the levels of stress and tension you feel within your working environment and – perhaps most importantly of all – increase your productivity.

Let's make a start!

In the next section you will discover the attributes of the various animal types we have identified. There may well, of course, be others in your immediate surroundings that we haven't identified so you can add them to your list – we have provided space at the back of the book for your own notes!

First
Take a look at the descriptions in each of the animal portraits and decide which best describes your own particular strengths and weaknesses.

Next
Turn to the **Talking Turkey Toolkit** where you will find information, questions, exercises and guidance which will give you valuable insights into:

- how to use this new found knowledge about yourself
- valuing your own skills both in the workplace and outside
- understanding your own position in the workplace.

It will also show you how to:

- manage yourself and your career
- manage your stress levels
- enhance your work life balance
- use the animal portraits to enhance your self-understanding.

What we are NOT asking you to do

Let's be clear - we are not asking you to make value judgements about other people around you.

This is all about you, your competences and capabilities, and helping you to understand how to balance yourself, how to allow your personality to shine in your own environment and, hopefully, how to derive the best results with your work team and colleagues.

We would like to help you not just survive but THRIVE in your working lives. So, let's take a look at those animal types!

THE ANIMAL TYPES

On the following pages you will find descriptions of some of the positive and negative behaviour traits of the 16 animal types we have identified as important in the workplace, along with their collective names and dictionary definitions.

Health Warning!!

Different people may see identical sets of behaviour and interpret or judge them in quite different ways. Personal perspectives often colour our judgements.

However, in this instance, the authors have taken their own view and are happy to accept responsibility for the various behavioural descriptors for each of the animal types.

DINOSAUR

Collective name: herd / pack

DINOSAUR

di-no-saur

1 Noun: A fossil reptile of the Mesozoic era, often reaching an enormous size

2 Noun: A person or thing that is outdated or has become obsolete because of failure to adapt to changing circumstances

POSITIVE TRAITS:

- Were often around when the organisation was created
- Have been involved at all levels for a long time
- Have presence
- Do not rush into things
- Are keepers of the history, both positive and negative

NEGATIVE TRAITS:

- Are overwhelmed by events
- Feel out of control as they made no preparation for current events
- Are retrospective not forward thinking
- Are unable to change
- Have a tendency to become extinct as they don't see the threat coming

OSTRICH

Collective name: flock / troop

OSTRICH

os-trich

1 Noun: A flightless swift-running African bird with a long neck, long legs and two toes on each foot

2 Noun: A person who refuses to face reality or accept facts

POSITIVE TRAITS:

- Are able to move very fast
- Pack quite a punch if necessary
- Have a long neck which enables a sweeping overview

NEGATIVE TRAITS:

- Have a reputation for burying their heads in the sand
- Will run away when challenged
- Will not change at any cost
- Feel that if you ignore it, it will go away
- Are those at the top who have never been a worker
- Are often in denial

LEMMING

Collective name: Usually loners so no official term
but occasionally called a colony

LEMMING

lem-ming

1 Noun: A small, short-tailed, thickset rodent found in the Arctic tundra

2 Noun: A person who unthinkingly joins a mass movement, especially a headlong rush to destruction

POSITIVE TRAITS:

- Are brave
- Are risk takers – willing to jump into the unknown
- Are loyal to the group

NEGATIVE TRAITS:

- Have a crowd mentality
- Have a self destructive tendency
- Are still here

SHEEP

Collective name: flock / mob / drove

SHEEP

sheep

1 Noun: A domesticated ruminant of the cattle family with
a thick woolly coat and (typically only in the male) curving horns

2 Noun: A meek, unimaginative, or easily led person

POSITIVE TRAITS:

- Are placid
- Are even tempered
- Will take direction
- Support the flock

NEGATIVE TRAITS:

- Will blindly follow wherever they are led or driven
- Believe that as they survived it last time then it will be OK
- Are unimaginative

BEAVER

Collective name: family / lodge / colony

BEAVER

bea-ver

1 Noun: A large semi-aquatic, broad-tailed rodent

2 Verb: To work very hard or industriously at something

POSITIVE TRAITS:

- Are dependable and productive in the right circumstances
- Are industrious
- Will get on with it
- Are the solid centre of any profession

NEGATIVE TRAITS:

- Can cut the wood out from under your feet unintentionally because they are so focused on their task
- Are blinkered
- Are not very adaptable
- Cannot work without very specific resources

SWAN

Collective name: flock / herd / bank

SWAN

swan

1 Noun: A large water bird with a long flexible neck, short legs, webbed feet and broad bill

2 Verb: Move about or go somewhere in a casual, relaxed way, typically perceived as irresponsible or ostentatious by others

POSITIVE TRAITS:

- Are serene
- Tend not to panic
- Work hard
- Are protective of their own
- Maintain their calm under pressure

NEGATIVE TRAITS:

- Are loyal only to their own organisations
- Are blinkered to outside influences
- Can allow their loyalty to override their judgement
- If at the top of the organisation, lose sight of what it means to be a worker
- Are aggressive if threatened

VULTURE

Collective name: wake / committee / venue

VULTURE

vul-ture

1 Noun: A large bird of prey with the head and neck more or less bare of feathers, feeding chiefly on carrion

2 Noun: A contemptible person who preys on or exploits others

POSITIVE TRAITS:

- Will clean up the mess
- Will drive away other predators
- Are very patient – will await their turn

NEGATIVE TRAITS:

- Are destructive critics
- Have a bad case of 'what are you doing for me'
- Are negative stereotypes
- Can badly affect external perceptions of who we are and what we do

ELEPHANT

Collective name: herd / parade

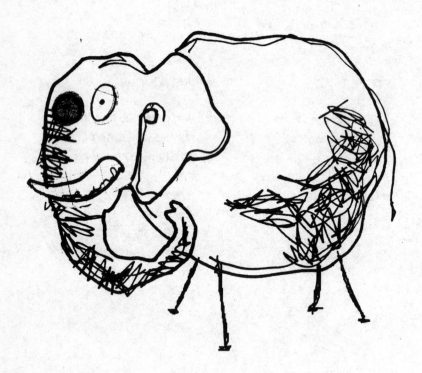

ELEPHANT

el-e-phant

1 Noun: A heavy plant-eating mammal with a prehensile trunk, long
curved ivory tusks and large ears

2 Noun: "white elephant" – a possession unwanted by the owner but
difficult to dispose of

POSITIVE TRAITS:

- Are supportive of
fellow professionals
- Are very loyal
- Are great at networking
for the benefit of all
- Feel safe in their belief
and structures
- Don't acknowledge
barriers
- Safeguard the 'wisdom/
knowledge'

NEGATIVE TRAITS:

- Will go off quietly
to die without telling
anyone they are going
- Are ponderous
- Can be linear thinkers
- Can go rogue without
warning
- Embed old ways of
doing things

MONKEY

Collective name: troop / shrewdness / tribe / cartload

MONKEY

mon-key

1 Noun: A small to medium-sized primate that typically has a long tail, most kinds of which live in trees in tropical countries

2 Verb: Behave in a silly or playful way

POSITIVE TRAITS:

- Work their environments
- Are inventive and adaptable
- Use whatever tools are at hand to improve products and services
- Are fun loving
- Are good to have around, great for water-cooler moments

NEGATIVE TRAITS:

- Can be destructive, often without meaning to
- Don't always consider consequences
- Will always allow fun to dominate over work tasks
- Have little respect for authority

LION

Collective name: pride / troop

LION

li-on

1 Noun: A large, usually tawny-yellow cat, having a tufted tail and, in the male, a large mane

2 Noun: A person of great importance, influence, charm, who is much admired as a celebrity

POSITIVE TRAITS:

- Are natural leaders
- Make a lot of noise (roar) if necessary for the benefit of both themselves and colleagues
- Provide the example of how it can be done
- Can drive forward change and innovation

NEGATIVE TRAITS:

- Are intrinsically lazy
- Will allow other people to do it for them
- Have an exaggerated sense of self worth
- Think they will get their own way if they shout loud enough

MOUSE

Collective name: mischief / nest / trip

MOUSE

mouse

1 Noun: A small rodent that typically has a pointed snout, relatively large ears and eyes, and a long tail

2 Noun: A quiet, timid person

POSITIVE TRAITS:

- Are hard working
- Can move very quickly
- Are quietly reliable
- Are not attention seekers

NEGATIVE TRAITS:

- Are timid
- Are easily frightened by the unfamiliar
- Don't like to stand out from the crowd
- Have a narrow focus

MOLE

Collective name: labour / company / movement

MOLE

mole

1 Noun: A small burrowing insectivorous mammal, living chiefly underground, with dark velvety fur, a long muzzle, strong forefeet and very small eyes

2 Noun: A spy who becomes part of and works from within the ranks of an enemy governmental staff or intelligence agency

POSITIVE TRAITS:

- Are highly focused
- Are determined
- Are tenacious
- Have a nose for sniffing out opportunities

NEGATIVE TRAITS:

- Live life underground
- Can't see the blindingly obvious
- Make molehills (or sizeable mountains) out of nothing
- Are subversive, going around stuff and then arriving in the light and surprising everyone
- Can pop up in the most unexpected places

HYENA

Collective name: cackle / clan

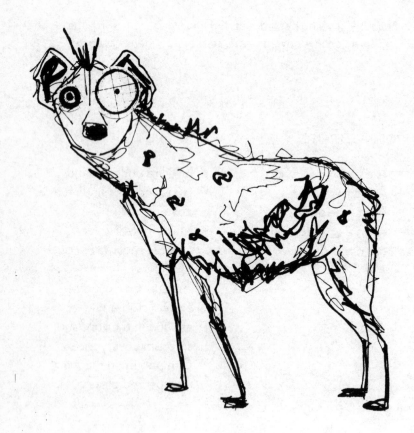

HYENA

hy-e-na

1 Noun: A doglike carnivore with a sloping back which feed as scavengers and have a characteristic shrill cry

2 Noun: Applied to cruel, treacherous, and greedy persons since at least 1670s

POSITIVE TRAITS:

- Are pack animals
- Are patient
- Are good to have on your side
- Enjoy company
- Are difficult to ignore

NEGATIVE TRAITS:

- Lurk in the background or on the fringes until you do something good/create something
- Watch you put in the effort but are not prepared to do it themselves
- Follow you around
- Don't create anything of their own
- Covet yours
- Steal yours or claim yours as their own

OWL

Collective name: parliament / stare / wisdom

OWL

owl

1 Noun: Nocturnal birds of prey having a broad head with large, forward
facing eyes surrounded by disks of modified feathers and a
hooked beak

2 Noun: A person of owl-like solemnity or appearance

POSITIVE TRAITS:

- Are wise
- Are keepers of the wisdom
- Are perceptive and highly observant
- Have very good vision

NEGATIVE TRAITS:

- Live their life in the dark
- Are loners
- Are happy living in obscure places

FOX

Collective name: leash / skulk

FOX

fox

1 Noun: A carnivorous mammal of the dog family, with a pointed muzzle and a bushy tail, proverbial for its cunning

2 Verb: To baffle or deceive someone

POSITIVE TRAITS:

- Read and understand the politics of an organisation
- Are community driven
- Are hugely adaptable to their environments
- Are not scared of change

NEGATIVE TRAITS:

- Are conniving, playing people off against each other, take advantage of weaknesses
- Are sly, cunning
- Can be scavengers
- Concentrate on the needs of the few rather than the needs of the many

DONKEY

Collective name: pace / band / drove

DONKEY

don-key

1 Noun: A domesticated hoofed mammal of the horse family with long ears and a braying call; an ass

2 Noun: A stupid or foolish person

POSITIVE TRAITS:

- Are very hard working
- Are reliable
- Take on a heavy load
- Are good followers
- Can be adaptable

NEGATIVE TRAITS:

- Can be dull
- Can be stubborn
- Can have a negative effect on those around them due to their miserable demeanour
- Are often imposed on but can reach breaking point without warning
- Can kick out if pushed

SO WHO ARE YOU?

Now that you have read all the animal types, we have given you a space below to note down your immediate response to the question:

"What (or who) do you think you are?"

In other words, which animal type or types best describes you?

I AM A:

```


```

With touches of:

```


```

And perhaps:

```


```

Now that you've got that off your chest, let's take a look at the **Talking Turkey Toolkit.**

THE TALKING TURKEY TOOLKIT

tur-key

1 Noun: large bird that typically has green, reddish-brown, and yellowish-brown plumage of a metallic lustre which is domesticated in most parts of the world

2 Noun: the flesh of this bird, used as food

Now that you have had an opportunity to examine all the animal types, it's time to "talk turkey".
(Dictionary definition: to talk frankly and practically; to mean business; to discuss in a straightforward manner)

The definitions and descriptions in the previous section should have helped you to examine your own characteristics and to be honest in recognising personality traits and tendencies in yourself - as well as those in other people around you.

But here is a big but - the only thing you are able to control in both work and personal situations is yourself, your own behaviours and your own reactions to particular situations.

You may feel that other people are behaving like square pegs in round holes or may display difficult combinations of character traits but, very often, you cannot do a thing about it.

Nobody else can govern the way you feel - just you. How you behave and how you react is about you and the choices you make.

This toolkit should allow you to establish what is helping you and what is hindering you in your personal reactions to your various work relationships. Then, as a result of that understanding, to find a way to handle the combination of character types around you.

In the following Toolkit sections we will be offering you some important areas to come to terms with / to understand / to deal with / to make some changes if needed. Here they are:

1   They're not the same as me – but that's OK
>   We offer you the reasons why we encounter different personalities at work and how best to work with them all

2   Ways to deal with the 'awkward squad'
>   We offer you some straightforward coping mechanisms for when the going really gets tough

3   Stress is both a workplace and personal threat
>   Pressure can be useful but stress is not so good. We offer you ways to deal with it

4   It is essential to look after your own wellbeing
>   It's not rocket science – you can't do the best if you are not feeling your best

5   Work / life harmony is critical and how to find it
>   Most things in nature work better in harmony and so will you

6   The pursuit and delivery of Excellence will pay dividends for your career and personal achievements
>   We tell you how to be head and shoulders better than everyone else around you

7   Why CPD – continuing professional development - is critically important to your future success
>   We help you to understand the benefits of being ahead of the game and being able to 'market' yourself effectively

8   The six questions between you and success:
>   We take a look at why it is so important for you to make up front decisions about your personal and professional development

Now let's begin!

1

THEY'RE NOT THE SAME AS ME - BUT THAT'S OK

 'As we let our own light shine, we unconsciously give other people permission to do the same'

- Nelson Mandela

So it seems that we have concluded that not everyone around you has the same approach to work or the same mental make-up, neither are they likely to behave or react to any given situation in the same way that you are. They are, in fact, a different personality type to you and, over and above that, will have alternative, preferred ways of working.

It has to be said, however, that just because they are different, it doesn't mean that this is a problem - quite the opposite. Working with people with different approaches to our own can be highly instructive. If we are prepared to take the time to see and understand the differences we will see why we are likely to achieve different outcomes if we approach everyone in the same way, without taking both our own and their character traits into consideration. It is also wise to consider that those individuals who display characteristics which we have the most difficulty in finding within ourselves are often the people who we consider 'difficult' to work with.

A very simple 3-step approach could bring huge benefits:

One- Begin by making sure that you are aware of your own chosen ways of communicating and behaving. Research suggests that a good understanding of self, both strengths and weaknesses, enables us to develop effective strategies for interaction and can help us

49

to better respond to the demands of our everyday environments. Take a look at the chart in the next section to understand how we identify our own characteristics. It also shows how others may see and interpret those same traits and behaviours differently when viewed from their own unique perspective.

 Two- Be open and understanding of the ways that other individuals may behave. Be clear that they act differently from you because their personality is different not just because they are being difficult! Also remember that 'them on a good day' may be radically different from 'them on a bad day'. Just think about how different your own reactions to a sudden problem might be if you are feeling relaxed compared to when you are still feeling aggravated about something else that happened earlier in the day.

 Three- Choose whether you wish to adjust your behaviour or communication style to fit with the other person's preferred style, to ease the wheels. Making the opposite choice may make your life more difficult or result in conflict.

There are perhaps three essential benefits to be drawn from utilising a more informed, co-operative viewpoint:

1 You could reduce misunderstandings and miscommunication which might in turn lead to a reduction in conflict situations

2 You will probably communicate and get your message or requirements across more easily

3 You might persuade the other person to meet you half way, bringing out a co-operative stance in that individual as well.

As a by-product you may well increase productivity as you will be spending less time 'dealing with' people and more time working with them.

DO WE ALL INTERPRET CHARACTER TRAITS IN THE SAME WAY?

As far back as the fifth century BC, Greek philosopher and writer Hippocrates identified four distinct 'energies' exhibited by different people. This was later the basis for Swiss psychologist Carl Gustav Jung to create his model of personality types in the early 1920's.

This seminal work on personality and preferences has been adopted and studied to the present day. The diagrams below illustrate the four personality variants and their so-called colour type descriptors.

BLUE	RED
GREEN	YELLOW

Character trait analysis also places people in two intersecting ranges:

- whether they are more introvert or extravert
- whether they are more task or people oriented.

The resulting groupings are often described by their four colour types and are thought to have a specific set of attributes. Analyses of individual members of staff within an organisation are often used by performance coaches and leadership training organisations as the basis for determining the root of interactions and difficulties within organisations.

	Introvert	Extrovert
Task	BLUE Perfectionists, love detail, avoid confrontation	RED Forceful, impatient, goal-oriented, need a challenge
People	GREEN Patient, reliable, good team worker	YELLOW Enthusiastic, like popularity, heart rules head

There are an enormous number of characteristics which will combine and contribute to any one individual being considered to be one colour type rather than another. For this reason it is so easy to make the fatal mistake of assuming that other people will interpret your behaviour in the same way that you intended it. The following chart illustrates how easily misunderstandings can arise:

	Characteristic we think we are displaying:	Others may interpret this characteristic as:
Blue	Precise	Cold
	Cautious	Stuffy
	Analytical	Reserved
	Deliberate	Indecisive
	Questioning	Suspicious
Red	Driver	Driving
	Purposeful	Intolerant
	Determined	Aggressive
	Competitive	Controlling
	Strong-willed	Overbearing
Green	Encouraging	Stubborn
	Amiable	Plodding
	Relaxed	Reliant
	Patient	Docile
	Caring	Bland
Yellow	Demonstrative	Flamboyant
	Enthusiastic	Indiscreet
	Persuasive	Excitable
	Dynamic	Frantic
	Sociable	Hasty

So how will you make sure that these misunderstandings of your own behaviour do not occur?

Wherever possible, be clear about your intentions and make your words and body language precise and unambiguous.

The perils of misreading a colleague's character have recently been highlighted by Susan Cain in her book *"Quiet: the power of introverts in a world that can't stop talking".* She maintains that at least one-third of the people we know are introverts. They are the ones who prefer listening to speaking; who innovate and create but dislike self-promotion; who favor working on their own over working in teams and to whom we owe many of the great contributions to society. She maintains that it is important to realise that not all noisy people are extrovert and not all quiet people are introvert and that these characteristics can be used as a disguise to mask other issues.

HOW TO SPOT A DINOSAUR

2

WAYS TO DEAL WITH THE 'AWKWARD SQUAD'

'God grant me the serenity to accept the things I cannot change, the courage to change the things I can, and the ability to hide the bodies of the people that really tick me off'

- Unknown

WHO ARE THEY?

Having offered you both positive and negative traits for all the animal types listed perhaps it would be disingenuous to ignore the fact that some of these traits can cause real difficulties in the workplace, however hard we try to accommodate them. It is difficult to generalise but most organisations can produce one or two employees whose life's work is to be as awkward as possible under any or all circumstances.

Working with difficult people, whether they are colleagues or customers, is one of the challenges we all share at work. They come in all shapes and varieties and can be difficult or negative, sometimes irrational or even intimidating in the way that they deal with us. You might come across:

- The bullies and tyrants
- The aggressors
- The mean and moody
- The churlish
- The overly competitive
- The control freaks
- The angry employee
- The incandescent customer

The types of behaviours you might encounter include:

- Those whose response is always rude and uncooperative
- Those who interrupt or pay no attention at meetings
- Those who take credit when they have contributed little or nothing
- Those who insist on telling you what to do without giving you a chance
- Those who bend the 'truth' to suit themselves
- Those who always appear to be in competition when what you need is some cooperation
- Those who are rude about colleagues behind their backs
- Those who are not interested in reality, just their perception of it

This is not an exclusive list – you are probably able to think of several other types of behaviours which make your toes curl. The problem is that, if left unresolved, these behaviours can become incredibly distracting and can take up much of your valuable time. They are also unbelievably corrosive to relationships if left unchecked over a long period.

Conflict and tension due to difficult behaviour is one of the major factors in poor performance, both for individuals and in the workplace in general. Your time, energy and sense of wellbeing can be badly affected by these difficult situations and can leave you distracted, feeling undermined or unable to concentrate on the tasks at hand.

SO HOW DO YOU DEAL WITH THEM?

The most appropriate strategy could vary from case to case and we offer some possibilities below but, in the main, the best advice is to remain calm and not get sucked into the scary vortex of emotion and negativity that these difficult people can create around them.

In the first instance it will always pay you dividends to just step back and try and see the situation from a different perspective, seeing the world from the other person's point of view. If you are feeling annoyed or victimised then this advice may feel counter-intuitive but it may help you to understand what the problem is and assist you in dealing with the behaviours which are causing the issues. This does not, of course, mean that you need to agree with the other person's worldview and how they are behaving but it may aid you in figuring out if they have what may be, to them, a valid reason for their behaviour.

Depending on circumstances, there are several differing strategies which you could employ one at a time or in combination in handling, dealing with or avoiding these problems:

✓ Always remain calm and positive, use your smile, welcoming body language and find words that will damp down the emotion - try and take the steam out of any negative situation

✓ Ignore it or learn to live with it. Most people will have some good qualities to go with their bad stuff so try and unearth those

✓ Invent practical workarounds. Communicate virtually, by email or on paper, in order to eliminate the face-to-face moments. This is particularly useful for individuals who are unlikely to be around for very long, e.g. temporary staff or those involved in short term projects

✓ Focus on the issue not the person. Try to shift any conversation away from a catalogue of complaints or negativity to a 'we-can-solve-this-problem' attitude. If you promise to follow up or investigate something then be sure you do so rather than risking a re-run of a difficult encounter

✓ Using basic negotiation and persuasion techniques could be useful in finding a way to achieve a mutually acceptable result for particular issues or problems

✓ Try your very best to stay away from office politics and personality assassination discussions. Hasty comments have an uncanny way of getting back to the person they were aimed at. You will not want any unconsidered comment of yours to fuel the problem

✓ If things truly become unbearable then let the other person know how their behaviour is affecting you. Obviously this would need to be handled with great caution and delicacy. Utilising the techniques recommended for delivering other types of feedback may be useful at this point

✓ Try to find some commonality with the person causing your issues. If you can find a neutral, mutual interest then conversations could become a little easier and may lead to overall improvement in the relationship

✓ Ask yourself if you are doing anything that may be causing the problem. A little honest introspection will probably tell you that you are not perfect either. If you need to amend any of your own behaviours then perhaps this might have a positive effect

✓ Always behave professionally and set the work tone at a level which you are expecting from the other person. In that way you have done your best to convey what acceptable behaviour looks like and it may be sufficient to prevent the relationship from deteriorating further.

WHAT IF IT'S THE BOSS THAT'S DIFFICULT?

It would be a rare thing to be able to choose your boss – they usually come with the job – but you do still have one choice. That is how you choose to work together. Their primary function is not really to make sure that you are happy – although you would want an enlightened boss to make some efforts in that direction. However, as we spend such a large proportion of our time at work they are going to have a big influence on our lives. So it is as well to remember that it is probably a good idea to make sure that the relationship is successful.

So if you have worked out that your current difficulties are stemming from the fact that your boss is a bit on the difficult side, how are you going to go about making the best of the situation?

- View the relationship as a challenge rather than a problem

- Don't get into any sort of power struggle – the boss wins every time and also holds the reins in terms of performance appraisal and references for any future potential bosses

- As we've mentioned before, the only part of any issue over which you have any control is your own. Try and see any issues in the relationship from your boss's perspective and do something which fixes the perceived problem

- Never criticise your boss behind their back. Negative comments of that type have an uncanny way of getting back. This will ruin any vestige of trust that you may have had between you

- If things are getting really uncomfortable, set up a private meeting to air your issues, ensuring that you avoid accusations that the problem is of their making. Aim for a solution that suits both of you

- Be generous in appreciating anything that your boss does which makes your job better or easier in any way.

BUT I'M JUST ANGRY AND THIS IS A CRISIS!

Even if you have tried all the techniques we have offered sometimes things can get away from you and you just have to admit that you are feeling incredibly angry. This is often the result of workplace stress and we will be addressing the issue in a later chapter but for now let's just acknowledge that difficult workplace situations can goad an individual beyond their normal limits, especially if they are feeling irritable and their usual tolerance levels have been negatively affected by experiencing unacceptable levels of aggravation. Anger is a perfectly natural response to a seemingly impossible or untenable situation.

Just occasionally anger can be a really useful emotion, motivating you to overcome what seemed like insurmountable obstacles when you were feeling a bit more rational. However, it can be very destructive if it is focused on people not problems. So here are some coping mechanisms which will help you to regain control quickly and mean that you will be able to get on with your day.

- If you feel completely out of control (before you react at all or utter a single word) take a deep breath, count to ten and try to remain as calm as possible. If this is really impossible then leave the room or the situation until you have recovered your equanimity and can respond calmly and rationally. If possible, talk to a neutral colleague first before you return

- Identify the source of your anger. Is it really the person in front of you who has triggered this extreme response or is it just the final straw? Are there other unresolved or unrelated issues bubbling away underneath?

- Focus on facts, events, actions, not on the person who has triggered your response

- If there is a need to put the incident on paper, write out your notes but do NOT send the first draft. Remember that other people are likely to read your comments so they should be as neutral and objective as possible. Give yourself adequate time to take the heat out of the situation. You do not want to embarrass yourself with immoderate language.

There are possibly going to be occasions when you may be on the receiving end of an angry outburst from a colleague. So here are some ways to reduce the negative effects of these incidents.

- Keep quiet and listen carefully while the person vents his anger. Allow him to finish so that he has got everything off his chest

- Don't use language that might trigger another outburst

- Maintain a calm, quiet posture and speak in a calm tone

- Validate his position and acknowledge his right to be angry under the circumstances

- Ensure that you confirm your understanding of the issues being presented

- Offer assistance, if possible, in helping them to deal with or resolve the problem. If that is not realistic then agree a method by which the issue can be resolved, even if that means involving a third party.

3

STRESS IS BOTH A WORKPLACE AND PERSONAL THREAT

'If the problem can be solved why worry? If the problem cannot be solved then worrying will do you no good'

- Santideva

In an earlier section we looked at how difficult behaviours in the workplace can lead to feelings that your time, energy and sense of wellbeing are being badly affected and how they can leave you feeling distracted, undermined or unable to concentrate on the tasks at hand. We may well define this as stress which is at an unreasonable level or having a negative effect on us. However, before we look at these negative effects we need to be clear that not all stress is actually 'bad'.

JOB DONE!

'To achieve great things, two things are needed: a plan and not quite enough time'

- Leonard Bernstein

For most of us, pressure is something we experience on a regular basis. It helps to motivate us and often assists us to perform at a high level. A binding delivery date for a particular project, for example, can keep us on track, provide the impetus we need to complete the work and ensure that we get it done on time. The resulting pleasure and pride we can take in a job well done and on time is important for our self-esteem and for how we are perceived within our organisations.

STRESS AND ITS EFFECTS

However, if that pressure becomes continuous and excessive then what we start to experience is often described as stress and long-term exposure can have very real physical and mental side-effects.

Stress is a relatively new word which has only been in use since about the 1930's and we use it to describe a feeling created by any emotional or physical threat, whether it is real or imagined. Most of us will feel stressed at some periods in our lives and it is often caused by a combination of factors in both our personal and working lives.

Stress can have both physical and emotional symptoms and, as we spend about 60% of our time at work, this can be an important trigger. There are some very common factors which may contribute to work-related stress:

- if we have unrealistic deadlines

- if we feel like we are in the wrong job

- if we have poor working conditions

- if we have an unsupportive manager

- if we feel generally undervalued

- if we find ourselves working with difficult colleagues.

In the current economic climate, normal work pressures are being compounded by 24/7 access to technology, job and financial uncertainties, as well as potentially unmanageable workloads. So those who are adding extra hours, taking work home or skipping their breaks are running a real risk that their willingness to try and stay in their role could actually be having a detrimental effect on their health and long term wellbeing.

MAKE IT BETTER

Relieving the effects of stress can be achieved in several ways, some of which are about the benefits of long-term good habits and we discuss these in the next chapter on maintaining our wellbeing:

- Liquids

- Eating

- Exercise

- Relax

- Sleep

It may take a while to establish the 'protective' effects and benefits which are so important but there are some other very practical things you can do which can have more immediate effects. These simple techniques can help you cope with a difficult moment or the effects which have built up over the day.

- Try some slow, deep breathing which is an effective way of bringing down your blood pressure and heart rate. Just close your eyes, concentrate on your breath, breathing in to the count of three and out for a count of six. Do this for a minute or two and you should feel the benefit

- Take a break. There is a very real temptation to work right through the day without stopping but this can make you stale or stop the creativity from flowing. You really need to set aside some time(s) in your day to stop and think or just relax for a few moments. Try making an appointment with yourself in your diary for half an hour each day. Take a break, take a walk, go and speak to a friendly colleague. You will find that the 'unwind' it gives you is very real and sets you up to be more productive when you get back

- Stop sitting! Two recent reports from scientists in the UK and Australia identified that we are under threat to our health if we spend too long each day just sitting at our desks, computers and televisions, even if we believe this is balanced by some form of exercise.

- Talk to someone about any difficulties you have, whether at work or at home. Explaining the problem and how you feel about it may help to put it in perspective. Getting someone else's view may give you an alternate solution or may just help by giving you the chance to 'offload'

- If you spend too much time worrying about things that may never happen or the 'what-if' scenarios, then you may drift into a very negative or pessimistic outlook which will create unnecessary anxiety. Try and deal only in facts and construct a plan or strategy that will help you to feel more in control

- Try to put a bit more energy into focussing on the positive things in your life. If you try and visualise a positive outcome, the more likely it is that you will be able to make it come true

- There is one final activity which can, if done regularly, shift your perspective quite radically and give you a method of bringing life's trials and tribulations into clear perspective and thereby prevent those little problem molehills from developing into stress mountains. Take a moment each day to remember the things for which you are grateful, the things which make you glad every time you think about them. Remember also to say a mental 'thank you' when something good happens or a personal 'thank you' if a good thing comes from someone else, whether it's a family member, a friend, a work colleague or a complete stranger.

	Three things that I am grateful for in my personal life:
1	
2	
3	

IN CONTROL OF THE WORKLOAD – IT'S ALL ABOUT TIME

If you feel that your workload is unrealistically high and your days are full of emails that need a response, reports that aren't finished and deadlines you haven't a hope of meeting then it may be time to consider one of the most effective of all stress eliminators – realistic use of your time, forward planning and getting organised.

There are some very, very simple strategies which will allow you to feel more in control and be realistic about what can be achieved each day.

- Get into the habit of planning your workload, not just for each day, but also by the week or month, depending on the type of work you are involved with. Take an overview of the total and decide whether there is anything that you can delegate

- Prioritise your most urgent tasks for each day and be sensible about how long each of these tasks is likely to take. If something is left incomplete at the end of the day then it automatically becomes your first priority to finish it the next day. Don't allow the daily interruptions to take its place

- Learn to say no. If your diary is full then you cannot take on any more, even if you want to impress someone with your willingness. Not delivering or doing a poor job because you haven't the time to do the work effectively is not going to impress anyone

- Keep your desk as clear as possible. Research has shown that working at a messy desk inhibits effective working and can create errors. Some creative minds may flourish this way but it does nothing for your ability to think effectively or find what you need quickly

- Take time to create effective filing and storage systems which will allow you to find anything you need without turning over the entire contents of your desk

- Last but by no means least - take control of your emails. If left unchecked your email inbox can be a continuous drain on your precious resources – your time and your energy. However, taking charge will pay dividends very quickly:

  - Turn off all sound and light notifications and bleeps to remove the distraction of new messages arriving

  - Decide on two or three specific times in the day, perhaps one in the morning and one in the late afternoon, to deal with emails and stick to them. Give yourself half an hour – you could use a timer – to clear as much as possible and then move back to other jobs. During these times concentrate fully on the emails and avoid multitasking. You will get through them much faster.

  - Avoid email being the first task of the day as the time you spend on other people's requirements and problems can escalate very quickly and before you know it hours will have passed and you have yet to begin your own day's allocated tasks! This way you avoid the 'What did I actually do today? scenario

  - Use your inbox only for incoming messages. Create a filing system within your inbox so that you can keep together any emails for particular projects, subjects or people, or articles and newsletters that you wish to come back to later, the choice is yours. Move emails out of your inbox into these holding folders. Watching people trawl for one particular message through several hundred that they are keeping in their inbox is the absolute definition of wasted effort

  - Email can create an expectation for immediate responses. Create some breathing space for yourself by sending back a holding email saying something like 'Thanks for letting me know / sending this information through and I will get back to you as soon as possible / in a day or two / when I've had a chance to consider your proposition'

  - Try to avoid sending any email message which looks like it might stretch to more than a few sentences. Pick up the phone or arrange a meeting instead and then you may prevent a whole email string from developing. Also, where possible, avoid copying additional people into the message to avoid getting dragged into endless 'round robin' discussions

- At the end of each day or whenever possible, aim to empty your inbox of incoming emails. You will be amazed how good this feels!

These techniques will easily turn into good habits and will give you the confidence to get through your workload at a sensible pace and the satisfaction of achieving what is required each day. This puts you firmly back in control and will automatically keep the stress levels down.

However, one of the key elements for maintaining our health and perspective is to take control of our own wellbeing and to ensure that we are able to balance the demands of our work lives with the benefits derived from life and activities outside of work – time to relax with our friends and family, our hobbies and interests, our ability to contribute to our communities. Most will describe this as the harmony which we should experience if our work and personal lives are balanced.

4

IT IS ESSENTIAL TO LOOK AFTER YOUR OWN WELLBEING

Self-esteem is as important to our wellbeing as legs are to a table. It is essential for physical and mental health and for happiness'

- Louise Hart

We said earlier that your personal reactions to potentially stressful situations or people and the way that you deal with them are the only elements of any interaction that you can realistically control.

A lot will also depend on the attitudes that you bring to those interactions and, in fact, to your work and life in general. In amongst those attitudes is one which has probably more resonance on your day-to-day experiences than any other – and that is the power of being positive.

Cope and Whittacker, in their book *The Art of Being Brilliant* tell us that their research into positive people reveals that they have several things in common and six main things that differentiate them from 'normal' people. One of those things stands out as being more important than all the rest. The number one thing that positive people do to make themselves happy, upbeat and full of life is that they CHOOSE to be positive. By actively choosing to be positive they are better able to attack issues with enthusiasm and are more likely to come up with solutions. But they do acknowledge that while choosing to be positive is simple, it is quite difficult to do all the time. They recognise that this is why most people don't bother despite all the evidence of the benefits to be found if they did!

Research from the Institute of Leadership and Management (ILM) calls this a key driver and a fundamental principle of work. When you feel upbeat and positive about what you are doing then you are more likely to raise your performance and ultimately to be more productive.

However, as we described earlier, the current workplace issues which are occasionally being caused by staff reductions, structural changes or carving out a niche for ourselves, can mean that our day-to-day environments are a bit challenging. Let's look at the ways in which you might be affected and how you can build up some resilience to the almost inevitable stress that we all encounter in the workplace.

There is a list of things that you need to do to protect your physical as well as your mental wellbeing. It is quite short but contains some really critical elements in order to avoid the detrimental effects that exposure to excessive stress can cause.

You should aim to:

Be positive
• Use your smile as your own personal secret weapon. As you smile and lift your cheeks this will tell your brain that you are happy. It also takes far, far fewer face muscles to smile than to frown!

• If you are feeling positive, happy and energised, you will be benefiting from endorphins running through your system and giving you an extra boost

• The more you smile, the happier you will be

Drink sufficient liquids
• Aim to drink a decent amount of liquid each day. This doesn't necessarily have to mean drinking litres of water as you absorb liquid from foods as well. However, it doesn't take very long for the body to become dehydrated and that will slow you down and affect your mood, probably also giving you headaches

• It is probably sensible advice to avoid excessive amounts of caffeine and alcohol

Eat sensibly
- The old adage of 'you are what you eat' has been shown to be largely true. If your diet consists of mainly refined and sugary foods then you are unlikely to be performing as well as you could and your moods will certainly be affected

Breathe properly
- Although we all have to breathe to live, a great many of us don't do it properly. We take shallow breaths from the top of our chest, especially at times of stress, whereas taking deeper breaths into our abdomen would be better for us. Taking a proper breath will help us to relax, boost our energy levels, control our emotions and achieve a sense of calm and peacefulness. Try these two different types of breathing

    o Full belly breathing - place your hands on your stomach and take a deep breath in through your nose. As you breathe in, feel your stomach rise then breathe out through your mouth. By doing this you open up your diaphragm allowing a greater intake of oxygen so you will achieve an increase in energy and vitality

    o 7:11 breathing – a great way to relax and calm the nerves before an important meeting, presentation, interview or in a crisis. Breathe in for 7 and out for 11. As an added bonus, the counting distracts your mind away from the problem!

Find time to relax each day
- If you can find time for some regular exercise each day, or at least two or three times a week, then this will help you to work off any excess adrenaline caused by those feelings of stress

- You might wish to try the benefits from meditation. Although most practitioners recommend meditating at regular times during the day, the bonus is that it is more than possible to find 10 minutes at time of need to practice your meditation to bring some much needed feeling of calm at a difficult time

- There are a great many other relaxation therapies, including yoga, Pilates and massage, which might be worth trying and you are bound to find one that you enjoy and which suits your lifestyle

Get enough regular sleep
- In an ideal world we would all awake relaxed and refreshed after a night's sleep and with plenty of energy available for the day ahead. However, the reality can be very different and it is possible that a great many of us are effectively suffering from varying degrees of sleep deprivation. It is very

possible to get used to feeling tired and we often don't recognise how our productivity and effectiveness are reduced when we don't get as much sleep as we need

- We all need a different amount of sleep each night and the odd disturbed night won't do us any lasting damage. However, we are all aware that we shouldn't drive when we are overtired as it can slow down our reaction times and our awareness levels

- There are some very simple things to do if we suspect that we are not getting sufficient sleep

- The most obvious is to go to bed earlier. If we have a regular morning routine and trains to catch then it is unlikely that we will be able to get up later as an alternative

- Try not to eat too late in the evening

- Try and keep your bedroom for sleeping rather than having lots of tempting gadgets to hand to create distractions late into the night

- If you really enjoy reading before sleep then try non-fiction rather than fiction. It will have a much more soporific effect

- Keep a notepad and pen by the bed in case those nagging thoughts are keeping you awake. Just writing them down will allow you to stop working so hard to remember them and therefore allow you to relax enough to nod off.

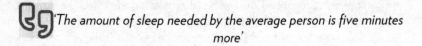 *'The amount of sleep needed by the average person is five minutes more'*

- Wilson Mizner

5

WHY WORK / LIFE HARMONY IS CRITICAL AND HOW TO FIND IT

 We continue to overlook the fact that work has become a leisure activity'

- Mark Abrams

We've all met them, those thankfully lovely people who will save your life or your sanity with a kind word or a smile at exactly the right moment. Then there are the other sort, the unpredictable people, lazy people, gossips, people that go out of their way to wind you up.

It is quite handy to regard these two contrasting types as pipes and drains – those who bring you good things (like clean water) versus those whose effect is to suck the life out of you. Remember what we talked about in the section on personal success!

IT'S A SEE-SAW!

 What you do speaks so loudly that I cannot hear what you say

- Ralph Waldo Emerson

Somewhere in the middle of this bizarre mix we all have to find our own ways of protecting ourselves from the extreme interactions which can cause our equilibrium to be well and truly upset. Losing that equilibrium for even a short period can alter our perceptions, making it easy to misinterpret what we see or hear or make us over sensitive to something which could really be quite innocuous if we were having a better day.

We talked in an earlier chapter of the perils and penalties of becoming angry and having to deal with that anger. It is also important to realise that two things can happen when our equilibrium is upset:

1 We don't see things around us as we normally would
2 People's view of us can get badly distorted

Either situation might badly affect interactions of all kinds. People's perceptions are incredibly important and they are constructed from a combination of what we hear and what we see.

Consider the following scenario. A colleague storms into the office. She is red in the face, tight-lipped, silent and not making eye contact. She hurls her papers onto the desk, drops into her seat and glares out of the window. "Are you OK?" you ask in an effort to be helpful. Her response comes back as a snarl "I'm fine!". What are you going to believe, what you hear or what you see? In this particular instance, her non-verbal behaviour – what you see – is so clear that you would be more than justified in not believing what she says.

Now consider this alternate scenario. You arrive in the office and your colleague is already in and working. When you say good morning she is uncharacteristically quiet in her response. When challenged she says 'Oh sorry, I was concentrating on what I was doing'. A little harder isn't it? Is she actually upset about something that has happened overnight or, in fact, concentrating completely on what she is doing? If it is the former then there is a lot going on in her head and the possibility for misunderstandings is fairly good. You might also interpret her reticence as an offhand response. You might then consider that she is being rude to you and regard it as a personal slight rather than what it actually is - a result of her being upset about something which might be affecting her normal behaviour. In this instance your perceptions are putting your interpretations ahead of what might actually be the reality in this case.

This is difficult turf to get right all the time and requires the deployment of a certain amount of empathy, an understanding of what it might be like to be in that person's shoes at this particular moment. Empathy is a really wonderful skill for each of us to develop. Admittedly some of us are better at it than others but it is well worth the effort of working on it to improve our ability to be someone who is prepared to suspend judgement long enough to get to the bottom of a perceived issue.

CREATING THE BALANCE

We know that recent surveys have shown that between 25% and 50% of people in the UK workforce report feeling overwhelmed or burned out at work.

If you feel that perhaps things are a little out of kilter in favour of your work commitments then here is our suggestion to help you examine the issues that may be making things difficult for you.

The following short exercise can help you to examine and perhaps shift your current emphasis and, by doing so, create a bit more harmony between the work and personal elements of your life.

We've listed some statements below to help you think about whether your work / life balance needs some repair work.

For each of the following questions make an honest response (try not to over-think them) and decide which of these three possible answers applies in each case:

A - Hardly ever

B - Some of the time

C - Most of the time

		ANSWER
1	I work for long periods without taking a break	
2	I am thinking about the next task, even while I'm still on the current one	
3	I say yes to things because people might be disappointed or angry if I don't	
4	I think about things I haven't done, even when I'm not working	
5	I say yes to things but I should really say no because I know I already have enough to do	
6	I am subject to emotional outbursts when things go wrong	
7	I feel frustrated and impatient although I try not to show it	
8	I feel guilty if I am not actually doing something	
9	Sunday evening is ruined because I am thinking about what Monday will bring	
10	My shoulders are hunched. I walk with my head down	
11	I work in the evening and sometimes at the weekend	
12	I tend to be ahead of myself, with my mind on the next task even while I tackle my current task	
13	I take everything very seriously, often failing to see the funny or lighter side of life	
14	I dream of escaping to a different type of life	

Total 'A' answers =

Total 'B' answers =

Total 'C' answers =

SCORING

Now we need to try and make some sense of your answers by comparing how many answers you scored as 'A' or 'B' or 'C'.

If you have scored mostly **A - Hardly Ever** scores, the better your balance so well done on keeping things in perspective and valuing the harmony between your work and personal life.

If you have scored mostly **B - Some of the Time** scores, the more you are likely to be somewhat out of balance and might need to change a few things to get back on the right track for bringing more harmony into your life.

If you have scored mostly **C - Most of the Time** scores, then it is definitely time to make some changes to re-align the balance between the personal and work areas of your life. It is time to invest in **you** in order to bring harmony back into your life and put your own wellbeing at the top of your personal agenda.

HOW TO MAKE SOME IMPROVEMENTS

Spend a few moments thinking about the questions we asked and the answers you gave in the previous exercise. If your scores have shown that making some changes could improve things, then the next part of the exercise could make a critical difference.

Begin by checking out the 'Simple Changes' section below then make some decisions about which of these and other changes might be appropriate for you to make and enter them in the grid which follows the section.

There are some fairly simple and easy to implement ways to have a quick and direct impact on how you separate your work and personal lives and make them complement each other.

SIMPLE CHANGES

Here are some very simple ways to make a positive impact on the balance between work, home life and recreation. They could quite quickly make a huge difference and ensure that you are not working 24/7 to the exclusion of everything else in your life. This is particularly important if any part of your work is delivered on a freelance or self-employed basis as the concept of stopping or switching off can be completely forgotten in the drive to earn fees!

They include:

- Taking a break. It is not possible to work flat out without taking a break so make sure that you put break periods in your diary and stick to them. You could get up from your desk, take a walk while you have a drink or even go and get some fresh air. Making some time in the evenings or at weekends to do things which take your mind off work will be great too

- Try not to take work home. Make an attempt to keep work issues at your place of work and give yourself the luxury of 'time off'. Don't be tempted to mull things over all evening other than perhaps to make a short plan for tomorrow if it means that you can then relax

- Do not be tempted to open your laptop or read emails away from work. Separating your work and home email systems makes this much easier to achieve

- Do you have a hobby or an interest? If so, make sure you set aside some time to enjoy it. If you don't have one yet then there are probably things you have always wanted to do. Find out how to get started so that you can begin doing at least one of them

- Many research studies show how important it is for the brain to just have a rest. Our world gets busier every day so we need to make a real effort to disconnect and find time to relax. We all juggle too many things, not just work, so seek out moments of peace or solitude if you enjoy it. It is said that you can only have a breakthrough after you have had a break!

TIME TO MAKE THOSE CHANGES

Now here is that chance to make some decisions about which changes might be appropriate for you to make right now and enter them in the grid below.

Remember that the second column might include things which you personally could stop doing or things which could be handed over or delegated to others. You might also consider changing how you look at prioritising tasks in order to change their emphasis within your overall workload.

Things I will START doing to create more balance in my life	Things I will STOP doing or change to create more balance in my life

!!! REMEMBER!!!

If you have identified the need for changes then the most important next step is to make a decision that nothing is more important than actually **DOING** the things you have written down. You will need to be single minded and dedicated to the idea of making that improvement in order to see the benefits.

It would be a real shame to have gone through these exercises and then lose the will or impetus to implement those changes.

Have courage!

HAPPY AT WORK

'Success is getting what you want. Happiness is wanting what you get'

- Dale Carnegie

One last issue to consider before we leave the subject of stress is whether you are actually happy at work. Shawn Achor, author of *The Happiness Advantage*, spent over a decade at Harvard University, becoming Head Teaching Fellow for 'Positive Psychology'. His research, and later work with companies undergoing severe changes in the current economic climate, demonstrates that it is possible to create positive outcomes and greater success by first training your brain to be positive at work – remember the earlier section on positivity?

People who are happy in their role can often be described as thriving. They are satisfied, productive and actively engaged. Most of us think that if we work hard then we will be successful and this will make us happy. However, the research seems to show that we are viewing this backwards and that 75% of our job success can be predicted by our levels of optimism, our support networks and our ability to manage energy and stress in a positive way.

So if being positive doesn't come very naturally to you then you may be asking the question as to whether it is possible to train yourself and the people around you to be happier at work by having a more positive attitude. Achor believes that the answer is 'yes' to that question as long as we change the way we think about work, success and happiness. His research shows that our brains actually work in such a way that happiness fuels success. When our brains are primed to be positive, it helps us to perform better than if we are feeling negative or neutral to our environment. Work then becomes more enjoyable and rewarding and Achor calls this state the Happiness Advantage.

However, as we are all aware, being happy at work isn't always easy. We all have patterns of behaviour which have developed over time and may colour the way we view the world and it is incredibly easy to get stuck in these patterns.

For example, a tax inspector who spends all of his days looking for mistakes in tax forms is, in fact, more likely to come home and unwittingly notice anything which may not be right in his home life because he is primed to look for mistakes.

It would seem, however, that it is possible to do a little brain-priming to help us all to be happier at work. We can encourage people to look for the positives by doing some relatively simple things, some of which we have mentioned in previous sections:

o Doing one thing at a time. Our brains much prefer to concentrate on one thing at a time. When we try to do several things simultaneously – the dreaded multitasking - we reduce our success rate on all the tasks. So concentrating on one thing at a time will make us more productive, we will achieve more and therefore make us happier.

o Being kind to people around us. If we look for ways to help others then this can change the way we see the world. Empathy and altruism will also change the way we feel about ourselves. Moving from 'how is the world affecting me' to 'how can I affect the world around me' could be a small but significant change

o Saying thank you for a job well done or remembering someone's birthday can make a huge difference to their day and to your own

o Being grateful. Try to recognise three new things each day for which we are grateful. Be as specific as possible. The more we think of things for which we are grateful, the happier our brain becomes and the less time we have for thinking about problems and difficulties

o Taking some exercise. It is not news that most forms of exercise release chemicals (endorphins) which have a positive effect on the brain. Regular exercise should also, therefore, have a positive effect on other areas of our lives and are a great outlet for daily stresses and strains.

o Smile - it's contagious! When we see someone smile or yawn, we smile or yawn too. This is known as the ripple effect. Shawn Achor claims that this is relevant to happiness as emotions can be transferred in the same way. If you were to put three people in a room then two of them will eventually leave with the emotions of the one who was most expressive. Stress, anxiety and uncertainty are contagious and can spread from one person to another, as can happiness. This explains why negativity can spread like wildfire within an organisation. So try to create a positive ripple effect, training people to look for the positive, smiling and making eye contact with others, giving praise, saying thank you or giving positive feedback, thereby creating a happier and more successful place to work.

	Three things that made me happy at work today:
1	
2	
3	

6

THE PURSUIT OF EXCELLENCE WILL PAY DIVIDENDS FOR YOUR CAREER AND PERSONAL ACHIEVEMENTS

'We are what we repeatedly do, excellence therefore is not an act but a habit'

- Aristotle

When we wake up and get ready for work each day, part of our mental preparation is likely to be a desire to get through what we know we must achieve that day, running through the lists as we have breakfast, rehearsing difficult phone calls as we get dressed, having ideas as we catch the train. By the time we arrive at our place of work, we all believe that we are ready to do a good job today and, for most of us for most of the time, the effort and the results at the end of the day will be very clear and satisfying.

There may be moments, though, when we ask ourselves difficult questions. As we make our way home at the end of the day and we allow ourselves to begin to wind down, memories of the day may begin to surface. We might become aware of a little nagging doubt that perhaps we could have handled that call a little better or we could have crafted that email with a little more sensitivity........ Have we delivered at something less than our usual standard or simply just not well enough for that particular task? What could we have done which would have guaranteed a better outcome?

The good news is that there is no need to be downbeat about these difficult thoughts. Instead give yourself a pat on the back for your self-awareness.

This inclination to indulge in reflective practice (the capacity to reflect on our actions so as to engage in a process of continuous learning) is an essential tool for anyone who strives for excellence on a daily basis. Why should we do it? What is it for? Overwhelmingly, it is because our search for excellence in day to day activities is not just about us and how we feel about doing our jobs but about the effect of our actions on others around us. Yes, we all need a level of satisfaction from a job well done but how can we 'guesstimate' the quality of our achievements relative to those around us?

The answer lies, to a large extent, in placing what we do in context and understanding the levels of interaction and influence with those around us. Even if your role is delivered in a predominantly virtual way, none of us work in isolation so our behaviours will affect and influence others in both expected and unexpected ways. The results of those interactions form the fabric of a jigsaw of connections which can tell us a great deal about our effectiveness.

Our daily activities are an expression of our professionalism and our delivery has an eventual effect, not just on the task in hand, but also on ourselves, on our bosses, our colleagues, the organisation as a whole, our clients and customers, the sector we work in and, eventually, society itself. We do not - and should not - work in isolation.

The big picture is, these days, a very hackneyed phrase and it is probably better to use the term 'contextual thinking' but it is still true nonetheless and should always be at the back of our minds, even as we tackle the most seemingly trivial tasks. We interconnect and influence in a variety of ways and at a variety of levels so the need for excellence in all of our interactions is paramount.

There is a story about big picture thinking which, whether it is true or merely apocryphal, is possibly the ultimate expression of the benefits of contextual thinking. The story is about a janitor whose job involved mopping the floors in the aircraft hangars at NASA.   One day, as he is going about his usual job he is interrupted by the arrival of a large group of visiting dignitaries. When one of them asks the janitor what he is doing there his response is 'I'm helping to put a man on the moon'. Now there is a man who not only has a personal role but understands completely the purpose and eventual achievement for what he is undertaking. No guesswork required!

'Excellence is not a skill. It is an attitude'

- Ralph Marston

'Productivity is never an accident. It is always the result of a commitment to excellence, intelligent planning and focused effort'

- Paul J. Meyer

7

WHY CPD - CONTINUING PROFESSIONAL DEVELOPMENT – IS CRITICALLY IMPORTANT TO YOUR FUTURE SUCCESS

The key to success is to focus our conscious mind on things we desire not things we fear'

- Brian Tracy

There are many reasons why CPD (continuing professional development) is critically important to your future career success and why adopting its requirements as a lifelong good habit will ensure that you are:

o always aware of new or important developments in your chosen field

o always looking for ways to improve your skills and competences

o always ready to take advantage of any opportunities which you may create or which may come your way through networking, serendipity, or just plain hard work.

There cannot be many of us who, hand on heart, could say that our skillset is so advanced or complete that there is no need for refreshing the competences we have or seeking to identify any gaps which need filling and which would make us more rounded professionals in our chosen fields.

I know that I would prefer to be treated by a doctor who had undergone some recent 'refreshment' of his skills than one who learned his trade 40 years ago and hadn't read or tried to update to new skills since then! It might also be handy if your legal advice was coming from someone who was aware of recent changes in the law..........

LET'S START WITH A SIMPLE CPD TOP TEN

1 It can be known as 'Continuing Professional Development'
OR 'Career Progression and Development'
OR 'Career Planning and Development' – this description may offer a more precise understanding of the major benefit of CPD

2 Most professional membership bodies are committed to CPD for all their members

3 Acquiring the benefits of a portfolio (keeping all your evidence together in one place) will mean that you are continuously assessing and updating your skillset

4 Get into the habit of utilising toolkits to undertake a regular skills audit which will highlight any current or future gaps, thereby encouraging you to look for training or information that you may need

5 Make sure your CV is completely up to date. There is no way of knowing when your dream job will appear and you don't want to waste any time applying for it

6 Keep track of your achievements. Sometimes in the day to day rush we fail to realise that moment of learning or experience which gives us something new or unexpected

7 Analyse any training undertaken and keep notes. Occasionally we can be disappointed by the selections we make. If you make a note of your impressions at the end of the day/event then you may realise over time that a particular type of training is not for you. This gives you the opportunity to try an alternative route which may be more to your liking

8 Utilise your appraisal documentation. Not many of us actually enjoy the appraisal process but sometimes what we learn as a result can be very enlightening. Pay attention, especially to comments about you or your work from other people

9 Acknowledge your work-based learning outcomes. Personal or professional development is not always about the formal events. Those 'Eureka' moments at work when a colleague explains something we have struggled to understand are every bit as valuable as working with a trainer we have paid for

10 Make yourself marketable – know your true worth! Even if your job is still enjoyable, take a few moments every so often to scan the horizon, either within your sector or outside, to see what other people are doing, what skills they are using, what is coming along which may not be familiar to you. Stretching yourself can be far more motivating than getting stale in a job that has become too familiar.

'Do one thing every day that scares you'

- Eleanor Roosevelt

IT'S NOT DIFFICULT – HONESTLY!

CPD is a very simple idea at heart - the idea that we all benefit from ongoing learning - but it is easy to make it look or sound more complex than it really is.

There are only two questions which you need to answer in order to make it entirely relevant:

1 What did I learn (what are the outcomes for me?)
2 How will I remember it (portfolio, notebook, diary, online system, professional membership system requirements)

If you are not comfortable with the term CPD then giving it another name can also simplify things – career long learning, lifelong learning – it really doesn't matter as long as it is clear why the process is necessary and, more importantly, beneficial to you.

The academics have been telling us for a long while that professionals gain the most benefit from their professional development activities if, as reflective practitioners, they take the time to consider what benefits they derive from their activities. They also tell us that this process will collectively enhance the overall understanding of how these activities benefit any given profession as a whole. This is a refreshing contrast to those who believe that CPD is about acquiring points or just turning up!

So although the established view is to talk about using the traditional CPD cycle to organise your development activities – plan, review, change as necessary – our view is much simpler. **DO IT!** - whatever it is – and have a think about what you got out of it. If it was useful then that's great; if it might be useful in the future then park it for a while and come back to it. If it was awful then that's even more valuable because you won't ever waste your time doing it again!

One of the most interesting issues about CPD has always been the possibility to recognise something which may be useful in the future, even if it is not entirely relevant at present. Will you know it when you see it? Have you cast your net wide enough to find it? Professional conferences are a great place to open your mind and think laterally about what is potentially useful.

These days it is virtually impossible to blink without falling over some form of networking activity, either face-to-face or virtually so dive in and give it a try. The same rules apply, you might love it or loathe it but you will never know what you might find unless you participate in some way.

The mixed drivers of intellectual curiosity, enhancing knowledge and the need to remain up to date for professional and CPD purposes should be enough to also make you apportion a significant percentage of your time to reading as widely as possible. Once again, it doesn't matter what you read – books, journals, magazines, blog pages, and on and on – the choice is enormous. The critical thing is to make the effort to expand your horizons from your current 'normal', however slowly and however frequent the attempt, it is still valuable.

'CPD is about the individual. It is for the individual. CPD is about stimulating and facilitating individuals to learn .... Essentially it is about motivating myself and others to continue to learn'

- David Pierce

SO WHERE DO I FIND IT?

Those traditional CPD activities that we mentioned before, such as conferences, training and workshops, are perhaps the most costly in terms of time and resources. However, there are so many simple and inexpensive ways to actively pursue your CPD that perhaps the easiest way to demonstrate the potential range available to you is to offer some of these avenues as a list. Please remember this is not an exclusive or definitive list. We are quite sure that once you get into the swing of this then you will be able to add lots more.

In your day-to-day work:

- Involvement in the introduction of new (or changed) systems, processes and procedures
- Inducting and mentoring new colleagues
- Taking on new/different responsibilities & learning new/different skills
- Giving presentations
- Delivering training
- Writing instructions and procedures
- Involvement in projects (short and long term) or working groups
- Deputising for colleagues
- Secondments
- Work-shadowing
- Working in other sections/departments or on other sites
- Chairing committees or working groups
- Arranging networking events
- Participating in networking events
- Involvement in the wider organisation, e.g. through working groups, training teams, committees

Through formal and informal training events:

- Academic courses with a formal award, e.g. degree, post-graduate diploma
- Vocational courses with a formal award, e.g. NVQ, City & Guilds
- Achieving professional qualifications
- External short courses
- In-house courses
- Evening/adult education classes, e.g. languages
- Extra-mural courses, e.g. Open University

Via professional activities:

- Professional reading – books, journals, blogs, etc
- Networking with colleagues in other organisations
- Active involvement in e-discussion lists
- Professional discussions with colleagues in your own organisation
- Membership and active involvement in professional bodies and related groups
- Volunteering to serve on committees, getting involved with the hosting/ organising of events, etc
- Mentoring and being mentored
- Attending conferences
- Attending exhibitions and product demonstrations

Via "outside" activities:

- Parent/teacher committee
- Voluntary work
- School governor
- Trade union involvement (including taking advantage of training courses)
- Involvement in running clubs/groups, e.g. sports clubs, playgroups, car clubs, Scouts and Guides

The key thing with any activity is to REFLECT on:

- what you have done
- what you have learned
- how you have used the learning
- the benefits to yourself and/or your organisation
- how you can improve/move forward

One of the very simplest habits to get into is to spend a few moments at the end of every week, perhaps on Friday evening, jotting down what you have learned that week – and remember it doesn't have to be earth-shatteringly important!

Also remember to make some notes after completing an event, a workshop, a course, or any other structured activity. At best it will help you to understand whether you are well suited to that type of activity or it may help you to decide that it really was not of any value to you. One thing that you will definitely want to remember is whether you liked the trainer/presenter and whether you ever want to spend your hard-earned money going to another one of their events!

We all know how much easier it is to NOT do any of this, to take the easy route, but there is no-one else who can do this for you. Just committing a very small amount of time – even 10 minutes a day or half an hour a week – on any kind of activity is going to pay dividends in a remarkably short time span. If you commute by train, you could use the journey to read a journal, if you drive then you can listen to an ebook. In this particular instance, anything is most definitely better than nothing.

   'Nobody can go back and start a new beginning but anyone can start today and make a new ending'

– Maria Robinson

BENEFITS OF CPD FOR THE INDIVIDUAL

'The best way to predict the future is to invent it'

- Alan Kay

- Increased self-esteem, looking back on your record of achievements boosts confidence
- Potential financial reward - evidence of CPD might well support a request for promotion
- Helps with reflection and analytical thinking – about your job, the work you do and how you do it
- Opportunity to enrich and develop your existing role
- Career development – identify skills gaps and learn new skills to move your career in the direction you'd like it to go
- Encourages creative thinking
- Reflective practice helps you take control of your situation and could help to relieve stress
- Written evidence of your CPD helps demonstrate / illustrate your skills in a concrete way
- Other skills, knowledge, expertise acquired in other aspects of your life could usefully be applied at work
- Allows you to assess and evaluate your mistakes, any problems or perceived failures, in a safe way to enable you to reflect on how you might do things differently next time
- Your CPD written record gives a clear picture of your achievements and the progress you have made.

BENEFITS OF CPD FOR THE EMPLOYER

- Improved service to users
- Improved performance and productivity
- Potential candidates for promotion
- Visibility as an exemplary employer
- High quality staff
- A committed and skilled workforce
- CPD provides cost effective learning opportunities through sharing skills; coaching; mentoring; work shadowing

MUST I DO THIS ALONE?
FIND THE RIGHT MENTOR

Very few of us flourish in isolation. We are social creatures and even while at work we tend to search out like minded people or amenable groups with whom we feel comfortable.

Some of us will be lucky enough to find a senior colleague or sponsor who can guide our progress and assist us in our careers. Such relationships are beneficial for both parties in that the junior partner benefits from the sponsors long experience while the senior partner benefits from being able to pass on what they have learned. All of us can benefit from having someone to help us, someone we can rely on to be supportive but objective, to guide and possibly teach us what we don't yet know. However, picking the right mentor is the key. So much so that picking the wrong person can be a very limiting experience and prevent us from flourishing.

For those who are employed, it is perfectly reasonable to search for a mentor within our employing organisation. For those who would wish to find their support outside the workplace then finding a personal mentor would be the ideal situation, either on a voluntary or perhaps a paid basis.

In the world of business and entrepreneurship, it has been shown that the most successful people often have a mentor or series of mentors who have guided them at different stages of their careers. Indeed, the UK government's Department for Business, Innovation and Skills (BIS) have conducted research which clearly shows that new businesses which seek out assistance and support are 50% less likely to fail within the first two years of being in business.

Seeking assistance in this way is not a sign of weakness but, on the contrary, a way to find out the things it would normally take us a lifetime of experimentation to understand. Most useful!

There are some key qualities that you should look for in your ideal mentor. They should be people who:

- You consider to be a great role model
- Are more experienced than you, not necessarily just older
- Listen more than they talk
- Care about and value the relationship with their mentee
- Have a great attitude – positive, upbeat and optimistic
- Are honest and care about honesty in others
- Know how to give feedback, focusing on your problem not your personality
- Will act as a sounding board in order to facilitate problem solving
- Accept you for who and what you are without wishing to impose change on you
- Have time available to focus on the relationship
- Are concerned with your growth, making you think about your options and possible answers to your own questions

Finding a suitable mentor can take time so don't rush into a relationship without considering carefully whether your personalities will mesh. It may also be necessary to change your mentor at particular times in your career, perhaps moving to someone with experience in a particular field. Don't worry, you will always find someone who can help you, however temporary that relationship may be.

Don't be afraid to ask for help whenever you need it.

8

THE SIX QUESTIONS
BETWEEN YOU AND SUCCESS

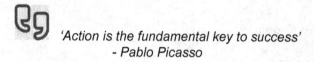

'Action is the fundamental key to success'
- Pablo Picasso

Up to this point, we have been clear that our personal choices determine what today, this week, this month looks like in terms of how we work with our colleagues. In this section we are going to take a look at what drives us to get up in the morning, how we determine what our career path looks like. Are we, in fact, the 'masters of our fate' or does our working life just happen to us when we aren't paying attention? Shall we start with the possibility that we would all like to be successful at what we do?

Success – it's an interesting word. The dictionary definition is "the accomplishment of an aim or purpose". But which aim? And to what purpose?

In order to answer both of those questions only you know what personal success would look like for you. For instance, would any of the following statements be part of your criteria?

- I want a promotion
- I want a pay rise
- I want to be my own boss
- I want to live comfortably
- I want to take a year out to travel

In many ways it doesn't matter how you define success. What matters is that you have thought about what you WANT and, by definition, what success means to you. Then you can make a plan to fulfill those 'wants' and work towards achieving them.

To enable you to move towards achieving your version of success let's start by asking six questions:

1 Who am I?

2 Where am I now?

3 How satisfied am I?

4 What changes do I want?

5 How do I make change happen?

6 What do I do if my plans don't work out?

All six of these questions seem quite straightforward. However, things are never as simple as they seem at first so let's go into each of these questions in a bit more depth and tackle a few exercises along the way that you may find helpful.

QUESTION 1: WHO AM I?

At face value this may be a rather simplistic question. We are all used to defining ourselves by a given set of criteria such as our name, our profession, our academic achievement, our family unit etc.

However, for our purposes this question is about looking past those surface descriptions and identifying who we are in relation to our personal values, attitudes, behaviours, personality, character; all of those intangible things that combine to make us the person we really are.

The 5 Words Exercise: Developing Your Personal Values

Personal Values are what define us as individuals; they are what influence our attitudes and they definitely determine our behaviours. For the career-minded, having a set of Personal Values enables an individual to have a more focused career path; for the business person they help to identify who your customers are, what you are supplying and how it will be supplied. So identifying your Personal Values is an essential task in both career and business development.

This exercise will enable you to identify your Personal Values.

1. Take a blank sheet of paper and brainstorm all the words and phrases you feel best describe you and your values; you may come up with things such as honest, trustworthy, confident, ethical, etc

2. Once you have all the words or phrases you can think of then go through the list again and look for themes. For example, honest and trustworthy are quite similar in meaning so if you had to choose one of them which would it be?

3. Continue to hone and define the list until you are left with 5 words or phrases that you are comfortable with and which you are sure describe who you are

4. The next thing you have to do is ask at least 15 people (preferably more) to give you 5 words or phrases that they would use to describe you. It's important that you ask a wide variety of people – friends, relatives, customers, business colleagues, your boss, someone you manage – as this will give you more of a 360° look at yourself and how you appear to others

5. Once you have both your original words and their feedback words, put them in the grid below (extend it on paper if you need to or download a copy from our website) and start to look for words that are the same / similar. What you are doing here is ensuring that what you think of yourself and your exhibited attitudes and behaviours match. In the end it's what we do (behaviours) that identify the real 'us' rather than our perceived versions of ourselves

Name:	Word 1	Word 2	Word 3	Word 4	Word 5

6. At the end of this exercise you will have 5 words that describe you – your Personal Values

My Five Words Are:

1.

2.

3.

4.

5.

After completing The 5 Words Exercise you will have a much clearer understanding of who you are.

The next stage in this process is to ask the supplementary question "Who am I, when?"

Over the course of a normal day / week / month / year we take on our different roles constantly, moving easily between: Child, Employee, Spouse/Partner, Business Owner, Parent, Consumer, Friend, Leisure-User, Home Maker, Student – changing hats as situations demand.

So when we start to consider change or moving forward to the success we have identified, it is vital to know who we are in relation to the variety of relationships we have because certain changes may have a direct impact on a number of those relationships. Having an understanding of what these are may help to highlight possible areas of conflict or tension – or potential help and support for your move forward.

Time Analysis Record

1. Write down as many of your current roles as possible in the Life Role column of the following grid

2. Next, try and assess the percentage of your time which you spend in that role. For example, as an employee you may spend 35 to 40 hours per week at work

To help you calculate your percentages:

There are 168 hours in a week, if you minus 56 hours (an assumption of 8 hours sleep per night) you are left with 112 hours. Therefore, 35 to 40 hours per week at work means that you spend approximately 35% of your week as an employee.

Of course, within that, you may also have other roles such as Manager, Supervisor etc. and this also needs to be reflected in the Life Role column of the grid.

We recommend that you carry out a short time and motion study on yourself over a two week period to ensure that you are not making incorrect assumptions about how you spend your time

3. Once you have completed the Time Analysis Record you will be in a better position to understand which of your roles is most likely to be affected by any changes you want to make.

This will enable you to make decisions about any compromises you may need to make in order to reach your future goals. Also, you can ensure that those affected by the changes you plan to make are aware of what you are doing, what you are willing to compromise and, importantly, that you will not let them steer you off course.

You are also, of course, hoping for lots of support.

Time Analysis Record							
Life Role	Percentage of Time Spent						
	10	20	30	40	50	60	70+
Example: Employee			35				

One more reason for considering "Who am I, when?" in terms of any changes we may wish to make is because different situations might call for some modification or enhancement to aspects of our behaviour, speech patterns, body language or even dress.

In the 1950's, in his book *The Presentation of Self in Everyday Life*, Erving Goffman described and developed the concept of Impression Management. His theory outlined his belief that, when we are born, we are thrust onto a 'stage' that is called 'everyday life' and as we grow we develop an innate ability to understand and react to the roles that are required to play - Child, Employee, Spouse/Partner, Business Owner, Parent, Consumer, Friend, Leisure-User, Home Maker, Student – which ensures we develop the skill of seamlessly slipping from one role, or persona, into another.

Impression Management sits at the heart of "Who am I?" and "Who am I, when?" By becoming aware of the variety of personas you currently use subconsciously you will understand the subtle changes you may have to make to develop the personas you will need in order to move forward and implement the changes to achieve your vision of success.

QUESTION 2: WHERE AM I NOW?

'If you don't know where you are going how will you know when you have arrived?'

- Anonymous

Every journey has a starting point; making change and achieving personal success is no exception. It is essential to identify your target – but you have to know where you are starting from. Hence the question "Where am I now?"

Do any of these statements resonate with you?

- I am bored and in a rut
- I know what I want but I don't know how to get it
- I want to return to a job after bringing up my children
- I am retiring soon and I don't know what to do
- I want to find out what's really important to me
- I am about to lose / have just lost my job
- I want to be clearer about where I go from here in my business or career
- I am quite satisfied with my life / job at the moment, but feel I may be missing out on something

Now it's your turn. Where are you are starting from?

So now that you have your starting point you can begin to create a list of the positive things you can take with you and the negative things you can leave behind.

You may have done an in-depth skills analysis in the past, or undertaken a SWOT analysis, where there is often an emphasis on the 'W' - the weaknesses element of the analysis.

In his book *Outliers*, Malcolm Gladwell explains the '10,000 Hours Rule'; the heavily tested theory of expertise. The theory explains that those we regard as experts or trailblazers are very rarely geniuses, they are more likely to be people who have put a great amount of time (around 10,000 hours over a fairly long period) into learning, practicing or doing something to the extent that they become 'expert'.

So, rather than considering your skills in terms of Strengths and Weaknesses; consider them in terms of things you like to do and things you don't like to do. The things you like to do, you are going to do more often and, as a consequence, become more proficient. The things you don't like to do you are always going to put second and, therefore, you will not be quite so good at doing.

Why is this important to your journey forward and the question "Where am I now?" Simple, your ultimate goal may require you to increase your skills in certain areas or you may need to develop new skills. If you discover the skills you need for success include those that you don't currently possess, you are going to need to develop them. If you find you need to do things you don't like doing you are either going to have to find a 'fix' or find someone else who can assist you in that specific area.

Skills Analysis

My Skills			
Very Competent	Competent	Want to use a great deal	Skills I would like to develop
		Want to use sometimes	
		Want to use rarely	

QUESTION 3: HOW SATISFIED AM I?

Naomi Campbell, supermodel, famously once said that she wouldn't get out of bed for less than $10,000.

However, research studies continuously show that most people rate job satisfaction, getting on with colleagues and decent treatment by their managers ahead of salary or receiving a bonus.

Our levels of satisfaction are influenced by having more, or less, of the things that make us happy. Making changes or moving forward requires some consideration of what drives us. Consider for a moment what makes you happy, what drives you, what gets you out of bed in the morning?

- material rewards
- power
- influence
- a search for meaning
- being regarded as an expert
- the ability to be creative
- a sense of belonging or affiliation
- being autonomous
- financial, personal, spiritual security
- status

Now write your main motivator here:

_____

_____

_____

_____

_____

Pipes and Drains

Having taken a little time to consider what makes you happy, what drives you, we can also begin to consider what makes you unhappy and what dissatisfies you. We often try to submerge those irritants but the good news is that once you name it you can start to do something about it. This is the essence of the Pipes and Drains exercise.

Pipes – bring good things, such as clean water
Drains – pull foul things down to you

Complete the grid below listing all of the people and activities in both your work life and personal life that satisfy you; then do the same with the people and activities that have the opposite effect

My Major Satisfiers		
	People	Activities
In my career / business		
In my life		

My Major Dissatisfiers		
	People	Activities
In my career / business		
In my life		

From this point forward it is your responsibility to ensure that you surround yourself with Pipes – those activities and people that bring positivity into your life; and steer clear of Drains – those activities and people that pull you down or sap your energy and enthusiasm.

QUESTION 4: WHAT CHANGES DO I WANT?

 'You must be the change you wish to see in the world'

- Mahatma Gandhi

Nothing is as certain as change. It is how we deal with it that makes the difference. If we know how we got to where we are today it will enable us to understand how we are going to get to where we want to be tomorrow.

Where have I come from? Where am I going?

You can do this exercise alone, but it works even better with a partner.

 One – introduce yourself as you are today:

Hello, my name is

_____

I am currently (job, business, school, college etc)

_____

I live at

_____

My aims are

_____

Two– mentally step back 5 years and introduce yourself, using the current tense:

Hello, my name is

_____

I am currently (job, business, school, college etc)

_____

I live at

_____

My aims are

_____

 Three– now step forward 5 years and introduce yourself, still using the current tense:

Hello, my name is

_____

I am currently (job, business, school, college etc)

_____

I live at

_____

My aims are

_____

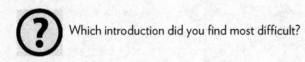 Which introduction did you find most difficult?

If the most difficult was introducing yourself as you were 5 years ago it may be because you have not maintained a record of your personal and professional development. The impact of this can be a lack of self awareness and knowledge of your true skills, strengths and abilities. We have already taken a look at this in the chapter on Continuing Professional Development.

If the most difficult was introducing yourself 5 years from now it could be because you have not yet fully clarified your goal and cannot, therefore, see yourself achieving the change you say you want.

QUESTION 5: HOW DO I MAKE CHANGE HAPPEN?

Question two asked "Where am I now?" and demonstrated how it is necessary to know where you are starting from if you want to make change; to move forward. In this question – "How do I make change happen?" – you can take a practical approach to forward planning in order to achieve your goals.

The purpose of planning is to set overall goals and to develop a plan to achieve them. It involves stepping back from your day-to-day operations and asking where you are headed and what your priorities should be.

Taking the decision to grow and develop means embracing the risks that come with growth. Spending time on identifying exactly where you want to go - and how you will get there - should help you reduce and manage those risks.

However, before moving on to the exercise that will enable you to create a truly effective five year plan it is important to stress the need to ensure that you are being **SMART**.

In order to move forward and make change your goals must really be:

- **S**pecific - does what you are doing take you closer to your ultimate goal; your 'big picture'?
- **M**easureable - how do you know when you have achieved what you set out to do; what methods are you using to measure effectiveness?
- **A**ttainable: can you do it and is it possible?
- **R**ealistic: realism doesn't mean being uninventive or unadventurous – give yourself challenges
- **T**imely: give yourself a realistic timeframe

Effective planning requires you to shift your focus from the day-to-day concerns and consider your broader and longer-term options. So next we offer you a method for creating a five year plan.

The Five Year Timeline

The Five Year Timeline is a method you can use to specifically illustrate and record your SMART goals over a five year period. It allows you the opportunity to identify what you 'want' – from work and life – in a way that can be measured, reviewed and reassessed as you move forward.

This is how you create your Five Year Timeline:

 One – complete column 1

In column 1 identify specific targets and strategic objectives. For example, the target 'Career Development' may have objectives that include job title, salary, a specific employer etc. The headings are entirely your choice as this is your plan. However, it is vital that the objectives you identify are as specific as possible and include measurable outcomes.

It is essential that you include one target heading for Personal Goals which should include objectives around home, family, friends, life etc - everything from where you live to what you drive – and you must not forget to make an area for home, family and life!

 Two – complete column 2

In column 2 you are identifying the point you are starting from – the way things are today. So, against each target, write down the current state of affairs. For example, the number of days or hours you work per week may be five days or 36 hours. Take a look at the worked example below; you will see that in column 2, headed 'Today', there is an entry which says 5 days.

Three – complete column 7

Rather than going forward from column 2, your next step is to move right across to column 7. In this column you should list things as you **want them to be** in five years time. It is essential that you are as specific as you can be and use measurable criteria. Taking forward the worked example from step two; in five years' time you may want to be working three days per week rather than the five you have listed currently. Therefore, in column 7, write 3 days.

 Four – complete columns 6 to 3

Now you need to work backwards from column 7 and complete columns 6 to 3. As you can see in the worked example, columns 6 and 5 show a four day week and columns 4 and 3 show a five day week.

The outcome of working backwards is that you are able to fully gauge your ability to achieve your 'want' targets as set in column 7. With this method you end up with five targeted, specific and measurable one year plans that can be reviewed regularly.

THE FIVE YEAR TIME LINE

Steps: 1	2	7	6	5	4	3
Criteria	Today	Year 1	Year 2	Year 3	Year 4	Year 5
CAREER						
Example: Working Days or Hours Per Week	5 Days					3 Days
		5 Days	5 Days	4 Days	4 Days	
Employer						
Job Title						
Number of Staff (Supervised or Managed)						
Budget Managed						
FINANCE						
Income Per Month / Per Annum						
Disposable Income Per Month / Per Annum						
PROFESSIONAL DEVELOPMENT						
Further Training / Development						
PERSONAL GOALS						
Home						
Car						
Leisure activities						
Family / Friends						
Holidays						
Pets						

QUESTION 6: WHAT DO I DO IF MY PLANS DON'T WORK OUT?

Let's face it – stuff happens! "The best laid plans of mice and men" and all that. But it is so much easier to deal with the rough of things going wrong if you know what the smooth should look like. This is why planning is so essential. Plans are not written in stone, they are a route map that can be adjusted or altered according to circumstances. Therefore, when things go wrong – and you can be certain that things *will* go wrong – you are able to consider your next options from a position of informed decision making rather than chaos.

It is essential to have a reliable, independent third party to give you help, advice, guidance, feedback and support. Sometimes this can be a family member or a friend – however, they are often not independent or impartial. Therefore a coach or mentor would be more effective. This will be someone whose advice and guidance you trust, who will challenge your assumptions and who will help you to see where to go next. Take another look at our chapter on finding a mentor.

Make sure you look after yourself in times of stress. Eating healthily, drinking plenty of water, regular exercise and rest and relaxation are essential. We have tackled these issues in our chapter on Wellbeing.

Do not be afraid to fail. Making change and achieving success takes time, patience and perseverance. However you should be very clear that you must make some time to understand what went wrong and, as a result, be clear about how to do things differently next time.

Think of the magic number: 5126.

Why is that number magic? Because it's the number of times Sir James Dyson *didn't* invent the revolutionary Dyson vacuum cleaner. Before the first dual cyclone vacuum cleaner hit the stores in 1993 there had been 15 long years of failure after failure. When asked about this Sir James said:

"Failure is interesting... you never learn from success, but you do learn from failure... I got to a place I never could have imagined because I learned what worked and didn't work."

So Sir James Dyson failed many times but still went on to become a phenomenal success because he had a vision of what that success was and a plan to achieve it. We can all do that.

'Success is not the key to happiness. Happiness is the key to success. If you love what you are doing, you will be successful'

-Albert Schweitzer

CONCLUSION

 'Wise people learn when they can, fools learn when they must'

- Duke of Wellington

This has been a brief and occasionally flippant look at some very serious issues which can affect our own wellbeing as well as those we work among. They can affect us as individuals as well as affecting our career aspirations, progress and levels of influence with colleagues within our own organisations. They can even affect the external perceptions of character and ability of any profession as a whole.

So we hope we have given you some useful tools which will assist you in reflecting on your current circumstances and in dealing with the daily pressures and personalities you encounter.

We would like to offer you one final exercise.
We would like you to reflect on a number of critical questions and to be as honest with yourself as possible.

We think this reflective exercise is so important that we have given you a place to write your answers in order to capture your instantaneous response. Remember, the only one who will benefit is you!

(?) What have I learned / realised / considered while reading this book?

_____
_____
_____
_____
_____
_____
_____
_____

(?) What actions or steps do I need to take?

_____
_____
_____
_____
_____
_____
_____
_____

(?) When do I need to do it?

_____
_____
_____
_____
_____
_____
_____
_____
_____

(?) What help or support do I need and where will I find it?

_____
_____
_____
_____
_____
_____
_____
_____

SO WHO ARE YOU NOW?

Congratulations on completing all the work offered by The Talking Turkey Toolkit. Now that you have arrived at the end, we hope you have been able to think about your personal characteristics and the way you work with people around you in new ways. So here is that question for you once more:

"What (or who) do you think you are?"

Has anything changed and would you now describe yourself any differently or do you have ambitions to be considered by others in new ways?

I AM A:

With touches of:

And perhaps:

USING THIS BOOK

This book has been written to provide you with a number of tools that will allow you to take a step to one side and view yourself, your interactions with others and your personal and professional growth and development.

Yes, you can dip in and out of chapters, pick and choose the exercises you do and refer back to sections as you wish. However, the best way to approach this book is to view it as a cycle of questions, exercises and activities that will allow you to take stock and move forward to your version of success.

THE WISDOM OF OTHERS

We all love inspirational quotes. Many of us have favourites that we have found useful in the past or which have helped us to find that extra ounce of courage or the patience to continue to the end of a difficult task.

There are an infinite number of quotes to choose from but we offer these and hope that you will find at least one or two of them useful in those difficult moments or when you need to feel a helping hand at your back.

All animals are equal. But some animals are more equal than others
- George Orwell, 'Animal Farm'

The Pessimist complains about the wind;
The Optimist expects it to change;
The Realist adjusts the sails

- William A Ward

There is no change nor improvement in this world
that does not start with the individual self
- Carl Jung

The measure of success is not whether you have a tough problem to deal with, but whether it is the same problem you had last year
- John Foster Dulles

It is not necessary to change. Survival is not mandatory
W Edwards Deming

If you don't like how things are, change it! You're not a tree
- Jim Rohn

Don't find fault, find a remedy
- Henry Ford

To solve any problem, here are three questions to ask yourself:
First, what could I do? Second, what could I read?
And third, who could I ask?
- Jim Rohn

Failure is not falling down, it is refusing to get up
- Chinese proverb

You don't get paid for the hour.
You get paid for the value you bring to the hour
- Jim Rohn

The greatest power that a person possesses is the power to choose
J. Martin Kohe

Man's unique reward, however, is that while animals
survive by adjusting themselves to their background,
man survives by adjusting his background to himself
- Ayn Rand

Working together works
- Rob Gilbert

Overcoming barriers to performance is how groups become teams

- Katzenbach & Smith

*Coming together is a beginning; keeping together is progress;
working together is success*
- Anonymous

*Isn't it funny how day by day nothing changes,
but when you look back everything is different?*

- C.S. Lewis

SUSIE'S ESSENTIAL QUOTES

On a filing cabinet in my office I have four quotes which I look at every day. They bring me courage and solace and remind me that there really is light at the end of any dark tunnel. You may notice that they are fairly eclectic and very, very personal!

Never, never, never give up

\- Winston Churchill

Life can only be understood backwards, but it must be lived forwards

\- Soren Kirkegaard

Live long and prosper

\- Mr Spock

Things are getting worse. Please send chocolate

\- Anonymous

KATHY'S ESSENTIAL QUOTES

My favourite quotes remind me that life is about doing, but also (sometimes) just taking the time to sit, relax – and do nothing.

Not only strike while the iron is hot, make it hot by striking it

- Oliver Cromwell

Today ain't over till tomorrow is planned

Anonymous

Insanity: doing the same thing over and over again

and expecting different results

- Albert Einstein

If at first you don't succeed, give up!

- Homer Simpson

AND QUOTES FROM THE VARIOUS CHAPTERS

Do or not do ... there is no try!

\- Yoda

As we let our own light shine, we unconsciously give other people permission to do the same

\- Nelson Mandela

God grant me the serenity to accept the things I cannot change,

the courage to change the things I can,

and the ability to hide the bodies of the people that really tick me off

\- Unknown

Action is the fundamental key to success

\- Pablo Picasso

If you don't know where you are going how will

you know when you have arrived?

– Anonymous

You must be the change you wish to see in the world

\- Mahatma Gandhi

The key to success is to focus our conscious mind on things we desire not things we fear

- Brian Tracy

Do one thing every day that scares you

- Eleanor Roosevelt

CPD is about the individual. It is for the individual. CPD is about stimulating and facilitating individuals to learn .... Essentially it is about motivating myself and others to continue to learn

- David Pierce

Nobody can go back and start a new beginning but anyone can start today and make a new ending

– Maria Robinson

"The best way to predict the future is to invent it"

- Alan Kay

We are what we repeatedly do, excellence therefore is not an act but a habit

- Aristotle

Excellence is not a skill. It is an attitude

- Ralph Marston

Productivity is never an accident. It is always the result of a commitment
to excellence, intelligent planning and focused effort

- Paul J. Meyer

*Self-esteem is as important to our wellbeing as legs are to a table.
It is essential for physical and mental health and for happiness*

- Louise Hart

The amount of sleep needed by the average person is five minutes more

- Wilson Mizner

*If the problem can be solved why worry? If the problem cannot be solved
worrying will do you no good*

- Santideva

*To achieve great things, two things are needed: a plan and not quite
enough time*

- Leonard Bernstein

We continue to overlook the fact that work has become a leisure activity

- Mark Abrams

What you do speaks so loudly that I cannot hear what you say

- Ralph Waldo Emerson

Success is getting what you want. Happiness is wanting what you get

- Dale Carnegie

Failure is interesting... you never learn from success, but you do learn from failure... I got to a place I never could have imagined because I learned what worked and didn't work

- James Dyson

Success is not the key to happiness. Happiness is the key to success. If you love what you are doing, you will be successful

- Albert Schweitzer

Wise people learn when they can, fools learn when they must

- Duke of Wellington

AND HERE'S A PLACE FOR YOU TO ADD YOUR OWN FAVOURITES

AUTHOR	QUOTE

DO YOU NEED MORE HELP?

If you would like any extra information about:

- the ideas in this book
- how to arrange individual sessions
- how to arrange facilitated group workshops for your organisation
- keynote talks for your conference or event

then please contact us at:

www.theprofessionalismgroup.co.uk/dinosaur

or email us at:

susiekay@theprofessionalismgroup.co.uk
or
kathy@kathyennis.co.uk

All of our charts and exercises are available as free downloads at:
www.theprofessionalismgroup.co.uk/dinosaur

It is also possible to arrange:

- personal support or mentoring
- group support or mentoring

Please visit our websites at:

www.theprofessionalismgroup.co.uk
or
www.kathyennis.co.uk

Further titles are due out soon from PROFESSIONALISM BOOKS
so do keep an eye on the website!

REFERENCES

There is a great deal of information available on the various theories touched on in this book and they are available from a variety of sources.

BIBLIOGRAPHY

The Happiness Advantage, Shawn Achor
(Random House 2010)

Quiet: the power of introverts in a world that can't stop talking, Susan Cain (Broadway Books 2010)

The Art of Being Brilliant, Andy Cope and Andy Whittaker
(Capstone 2012)

Outliers, Malcolm Gladwell
(Penguin 2008)

The Presentation of Self in Everyday Life, Erving Goffman
(Penguin 1959)

Professionalism: The ABC for Success, Susie Kay
(Professionalism Books 2010)

WEBSITES

The Institute of Enterprise and Entrepreneurs
www.ioee.co.uk

The Institute of Leadership and Management
www.i-l-m.com

Department for Business, Innovation and Skills
UK Government website
www.gov.uk/government/organisations/department-for-business-innovation-skills

AND FINALLY

"The only thing to do with good advice is to pass it on.
It is never of any use to oneself."

- Oscar Wilde

ABOUT THE AUTHORS

Susie Kay has worked for many years in professional associations and membership organisations, advising on the wider aspects of professionalism and professional development. Her experience of leading teams and the strategic management of these organisations has meant working with a wide range of organisational structures, cultures and stakeholder groups. These included the academic community, government departments and time spent working with international strategy groups addressing the issues around professionalism.

She is now an international speaker and author. Her previous book "Professionalism – the ABC for Success" sells widely, including an international edition in India. Her articles on professionalism and associated personal effectiveness subjects are published widely. She is a keynote and conference speaker and provides consultancy and workshops on all aspects of personal productivity and effectiveness, as well as being a registered mentor. She advises on governance and operational issues within the non-profit sector and mentors their Chief Executives to ensure the organisations remain successful and sustainable. She is a Founding Member of the Professional Development Consortium and an Expert Board Member for the CPD Standards Office.

Kathy Ennis is an expert in personal branding, visual communication and engagement marketing. As a mentor, trainer and public speaker Kathy uses this expertise as a method for ensuring business growth and career development for her clients. With over 20 years experience at senior level in the Information Industry and more than 10 years business experience Kathy designs and delivers mentoring, training and learning programmes to a wide variety of individuals and organisations in the UK, Europe and Scandinavia. Her public and private business clients have ranged from Specsavers, McDonalds and Linklaters to Breast Cancer Care, Enterprise Enfield and the North Wales Libraries Partnership.

Kathy works with individuals and groups of all sizes, as a mentor, trainer and as a highly effective and entertaining conference speaker. She firmly believes that it is individual effectiveness that contributes most to the overall success of any organisation. Kathy helps people grow their business; develop better business networking, public speaking and presentation skills; improve their communication and business relationship-building skills; build their confidence and self esteem; provide them with career enhancing interview preparation;

and develops their personal brand, the process of communicating through appearance and behaviour.

Rebecca Walters completed an Art Foundation Course at Camberwell College of Arts, University of the Arts (2005-2006). Her penchant for scribbling not quite satisfied, she went on to obtain an honours degree in Illustration at Lincoln University (2006-2009). Her favoured medium is pen and ink but she has developed an interest in using mixed media to create unusual and striking characters.

INDEX

FOR YOUR OWN NOTES:

FOR YOUR OWN NOTES:

FOR YOUR OWN NOTES:

FOR YOUR OWN NOTES:

ALSO FROM
PROFESSIONALISM BOOKS

Professionalism is a choice, an opportunity for you to think, behave and act in a way which will make you stand out from the crowd. This book offers you an insight into the ways that professionals approach their world and offers some very practical advice, intended to help you demonstrate your own professionalism 24/7

If you know that just getting by isn't enough and that there must be something missing – professionalism is the answer.

What do readers think of the book?

"It is not only a book on professionalism, it is also a manual for living"

"An excellent recipe book for professionalism - all the key ingredients are here at your fingertips"

"Practical advice which can easily fit into your working day and life. This book is definitely going on my bookshelf! "

Available from PROFESSIONALISM BOOKS, Amazon, Waterstones and all good bookshops